Liverpool River follows the world-famous River Mersey from its source to the heart of our city.

The Mersey has always been central to Liverpool life and here we look back at our great river through more than 100 newly restored photographs from the Liverpool Daily Post and Echo archive. This unique collection of images celebrates the vessels that have sailed from Merseyside – from the great ocean-going Cunard liners to the cross-river ferries we know and love. We also look at the people who lived and worked around the Mersey, how it has changed lives and played a major part in our city's evolution from a tiny Pool of Life to the European Capital of Culture 2008.

Liverpool River is sure to bring memories flooding back.

Why not contribute your own historic Merseyside photographs and memories to share with others over the internet, using our online People's Archive? It can be accessed by visiting the websites for the Daily Post (www.liverpooldailypost.co.uk) or Liverpool Echo (www.liverpoolecho.co.uk) and clicking on the People's Archive icon.

Alternatively, if you have a personal river story and you want to write to us: River People, PO Box 48, Old Hall Street, L69 3EB. Please note that by submitting stories/pictures you grant us copyright permission to use in any future Trinity Mirror publication.

Many of the photographs featured in this title are available for sale by contacting 0151 472 2549.

Above IT'S A LOCK-IN: The then HRH Princess Elizabeth and HRH the Duke of Edinburgh officially open the new Waterloo Lock aboard Mersey Docks & Harbour Board's directors' fine steam tender Galatea, with crowds lining the quayside, on May 30, 1949. Note the loudspeakers on Galatea's bow primed for the immortal words "Mae husband and I..."

WUTHERING HEIGHTS: The cradle of the Mersey starts high in the Goyt valley as the waters of Stake Clough cascade through this bleakly beautiful landscape

MONARCHS OF THE GLEN: Doubtless shepherd Jack Brocklehurst and his dog Laddie are long gone, but the waters that feed the Mersey still tumble down the Goyt valley as they did here in June, 1968

GOLDEN LINING: The sun breaks through the clouds, illuminating our great river

STRIKE OFF: No smoke-free city edict upsets this fine array of Rea and Alexandra tugs lighting up for business after a strike kept 17 of them idle in Gladstone Dock, Liverpool, in May, 1955

Top VANQUISHED AND CONQUEROR: Capt Gustav Erikson's fabled grain-carrying barque Moshulu is eased into Alfred Dock, Birkenhead, by Alexandra Towing Co's Bramley Moore steam-tug, watched by crew aboard the Royal Mail Lines' new motor freighter Britanny, on September 9, 1937. The acclaimed travel writer Eric Newby sailed on Moshulu to Australia just before the war as he recounted in The Great Grain Race, a fine epitaph for the last hurrah of these magnificent square riggers. Moshulu was spared the breaker's hammer and is now a floating restaurant in Philadelphia, US

Above STAGE PERFORMERS: The '60s start swinging on George's landing stage, Liverpool, as Gerry and the Pacemakers rev up their Lambrettas to film Ferry 'Cross the Mersey on August 13, 1964

Top MISSION POSSIBLE: With her engines throbbing, Flying Breeze turns towards the Mersey Bar on December 22, 1959 to deliver Planet's Christmas hampers, supplied by the Mersey Mission to Seamen, whose ensign flies from the mast (partly obscured by the funnel) which also sports a Christmas tree on top

Above SEASONAL SEND-OFF: Choirboys of St Gabriel's Church, Huyton Quarry, Liverpool Central Unit Sea Cadets and Flying Breeze's Capt Walter Roberts, dressed as Father Christmas, welcome the traditional yuletide hampers aboard Alexandra Co's famous tug tender at Princes landing stage, destined for the crew of the lightvessel Planet, moored at Mersey Bar, on December 22, 1960

CHRISTMAS CHEER: Capt Walter Roberts (still dressed as Santa Claus) expertly holds Flying Breeze alongside the lightvessel at the Mersey Bar, as the precious hampers are swung across to Planet, on December 22, 1960

Above WHAT A CLANGER: A Wallasey Ferries crewman grasps the clapper of Seacombe landing stage's fog bell, prior to its conversion to electric
operation in August, 1931
Centre WINTER WALLASEY WONDERLAND: Icicles turn the bow of Wallasey Ferries' Leasowe into a pantomime whale's mouth, in the big freeze
of January 1963, at Liverpool landing stage

WHAT A WHOPPER: IoMSPCo's flagship Ben-My-Chree (IV), of 1927, with her stupendous funnel (later cut down by 15') backs away from Princes landing stage, flying the Pilot Jack at the bowstaff. The only time a Union Jack was permitted on merchant ships' jack staff was when a pilot was requested, on May 19, 1934. The Ben sports her newly painted white hull (previously black)

Top TOFFS' TRAVEL: First class passengers sometimes embarked on ocean liners after they cast off and anchored mid-river. Here's the upper eschelon embarking on Alexandra's tug tender Flying Breeze at Princes landing stage, on June 23, 1955. IoMSPCo's King Orry lies ahead

Above THE LAST VOYAGE: The Mersey luggage boats, which appear in so many old river views plying between Liverpool landing stage and Wallasey were severely hit by the opening of the 1934 Queensway Birkenhead tunnel but, thanks to war work, staggered on until April, 1947, when SS Perch Rock closed the service. With her going another great river trade passed into history

VIKING WARRIOR: The prow of IoMSPCo's King Orry, like some latterday Nordic long boat, looms over the shipyard workers in Canada Dock adjusting her bow rudder as she is prepared for her final summer season on March 6, 1975, in this memorable shot by Post and Echo photographer Stephen Shakeshaft

COAL SHOAL: Steam tugs from Alexandra, Rea and Cock companies (note the latter's mast-top black cock weather-vane) forage around the coal barge and collier, far left, as they bunker fuel at Sandon Half Tide Dock, Liverpool, in March 9, 1956. The large freighter is Port Line's Port Macquarrie, and our old friend Flying Breeze is fourth funnel from right

NEW FOR NEW BRIGHTON: The £6,000 Edmund and Mary Robinson lifeboat arrives at Princes Dock, Liverpool, for hand-over to the RNLI, in February, 1939, with a British & Irish Line two-funnelled Lady-class cross channel ferry for Dublin and another fleet-mate lost in the gloom behind

Top   CAR FERRY: In September 1963 commuters, such as the owners of these once familiar Roots Group saloons – could still park for free on
Seacombe promenade and catch Wallasey boats such as Leasowe, seen sprinting away to Liverpool, to the office

Above   VIEW FROM THE BRIDGE: These faces etched with concentration show that river work was no sinecure. On the bridge of Wallasey Ferries'
famous "fish 'n' chip boat" Royal Iris are Capt E H McCormack, Mate D Barber and at the helm, leading seaman D Hazlehurst, in May, 1960

CHILD'S PLAY: Many people's lifelong interest in ships and the sea was kindled by weekend afternoons spent like this – walks taken as a youngster along Princes Landing Stage, the world's largest floating structure, just to see "if anything interesting is in". And there is – the salvage ships Vigilant and Salvor (whose funnel pokes up far right), in November, 1958

DROPPING THE PILOT: The great square rigger Parma unfurls her sails as one of Liverpool's steam pilot boats scurries away, captured here by Capt A Wilson, of the tug Alexandra, which has just released the tow rope in Liverpool Bay in September, 1934

Top BRUNEL'S VISION: IKB's 1860 Great Eastern, reduced to a static role as Lewis's department store floating shopping and entertainment emporium at Rock Ferry. Unsurpassed for decades as the world's biggest ship, failure as an ocean liner instead ensured enduring fame laying the first transatlantic cable and bringing continents together

Above FOND FAREWELL: Dora Bryan look-alike Dorothy Boote serves tea to these solid Salford matrons during the 1927 Ben-My-Chree's last voyage, on September 9, 1965. Note the fine panelling and filigree woodwork for which Cammell Laird's craftsmen were once renowned

BIG SEND-OFF: Well-wishers throng Princes landing stage as Cunard Line's 1939-built Mauretania enjoys a second maiden voyage from Liverpool to New York after postwar reconditioning, on April 26, 1947

UP AND OVERHEAD: Liverpool Strand seen from the Royal Liver Building's east tower, giving a gull's eye view of the Liverpool Overhead Railway, Cunard Building (far right) and George's Dock Vent (top right). The Goree Piazza warehouses (centre) still display wartime incendiary rooftop damage, likewise White Star Building (now Albion House), top left

OUTREACH PROJECT: The Runcorn Bridge's framework, seen from the town itself, stretches across the gap over the Manchester Ship Canal and River Mersey to its mirror image on Widnes West Bank in July, 1960; while the Transporter Bridge behind rumbles on to its destiny

FOG-BOUND: Winter sunlight breaks through over Cammell Laird Shipyard, Birkenhead, as cold air meets with warm seawater trapping the rising vapour in this spectacular Frank Loughlin panorama from November 1981. In the foreground Brunswick Half-tide Dock wheelwrights' shed emerges from the gloom as if an isolated island

Top WAITING GAME: a tramway inspector and driver stroll deep in conversation as horse-drawn trams and buses rest at Pier Head. The photo dates between Liverpool Overhead Railway's 1893 opening and the 1901 tramway electrification. Everything, including the original Tower Building, has gone except for Our Lady & St Nicholas's parish church tower

Above ALL ABROAD: Liverpool & North Wales Steamship Co's flagship St Tudno rounds the Great Orme to Llandudno – Queen of Welsh resorts – returning daytrippers to Liverpool from Menai Bridge during the Whitsuntide holiday of May, 1947

MERSEY SKYWAY: Two boys enjoy the view from New Brighton chair lift to the Tower Building, above a fairly grim scene in May, 1968, when the resort should be readying for the summer season. The Tivoli Theatre, centre left, looks secure but the pier and fairground are forlorn. In the background, drilling piles for Royal Seaforth Dock starts, later changing tide patterns and stripping New Brighton's sands

Top DRESSED OVERALL: Wirral's top drawer folk parade in their Sunday best on Seacombe promenade in July, 1913, for King George V's visit, with ships dressed overall in mid-river. Canadian Pacific's ill-fated Empress of Ireland, left, Brocklebank freighter, centre, and the world's fastest ship, Cunard's four-funnelled Mauretania, far right

Above PIER APPROVAL: Almost as smartly turned out (compared to today), crowds flock around New Brighton Pier and beach in August, 1950

Top FAIR WEATHER: Three children get donkey rides on New Brighton sands with Perch Rock lighthouse behind in June 1954, when donkeys legally had a shorter working day than men – and knew exactly when to knock off

Above FOUL WEATHER: A bit of a lump on the Mersey with Royal Daffodil (III) alongside New Brighton Pier (looking solid although the prom railings have taken a bashing) approaching New Year on December 28, 1960, by Harold Clough

Top RIP: Many people thought the end was nigh for Albert Dock as shown here by Stephen Shakeshaft in February 1976, before its transformation into a tourist attraction

Above SOUTHERLY ASPECT: A panoramic view by Derek Wright of Liverpool's South End Docks, busy in February 1980, with the great Brunswick Dock grain silo, bottom right, and IoMSPCo's little cargo boat Peveril (built 1963) front centre, in Coburg Dock (from which Cunard Line's first transatlantic mail steamer Britannia departed in 1840); then, northwards, Queen's, King's, Wapping, Salthouse, Canning and Pier Head, top

CHRISTMAS SAIL: Shaw Savill & Albion's Alaric and a Port Line cargoliner load up at the Dowie berth for the colonies (aka "pneumonia corner") alongside Gladstone Dock west side, on October 26, 1970. These were the "Christmas boats" for Australasia, arriving in December. Dumper trucks and crates of Rover parts marked SYD for Sydney, NSW, await transhipment in the days when we had an exporting engineering industry

Top POKER FACES: Dockers smile broadly for Stephen Shakeshaft in the B&I Line ro-ro berth's café at Waterloo Dock, Liverpool, appearing to be taking a break from their preferred brag for poker. They can't all be winning

Above BRIDGE VIEW: Guided by two Alexandra tugs, Canadian Pacific's new Empress of England locks out of Gladstone Dock en route to Princes landing stage, in April 1957, by Walter McEvoy

BUOYS' OWN WORLD: Channel buoys under repair with the two famous Mersey vessels, Salvor and Vigilant, behind, which in the days of Liverpool's greatness were fully-occupied tending buoys and conservancy, tasks now undertaken by floating crane Mersey Mammoth

LIGHTEN THEIR DARKNESS: Dockers and electric trolleys move around Clan Line's gloomy Vittoria Dock warehouse, Birkenhead, in this George Fisher image

DAVID AND GOLIATH: A tiny gig boat crewed by boatmen Charlie Nelson and Stanley Gray takes mooring lines from South American Saint Line's freighter St Merriel, formerly Houlder Bros'Thorpe Grange (both part of Furness group) as the 6,695-ton vessel moves from Hornby to Alexandra Dock, in October, 1966

GRAVE SIGHT: Gladstone Graving Dock in December, 1962, with a Blue Star cargo-liner behind in "pneumonia corner". Blocks are being prepared for an incoming ship so shoring is not needed between the walls and hull sides

Top SKY TRAIN: The world's most famous steam locomotive Flying Scotsman lives up to its name while being unloaded by floating crane Mammoth from Cunard's Saxonia after rescue by William McAlpine from an ill-fated US tour in February, 1973

Above WATERFRONT LIVING: Alec Morris, charge-hand water runner (Hornby Lock caretaker), with Mrs Morris and their dog, look sceptically out from their Mersey Docks & Harbour Board house, in April, 1967. A Brocklebank freighter, left, locks in, with the Blue Funnel Line shed in South Gladstone No 1 Branch Dock behind

Top WAREHOUSE WORLD: This August 1956 Dock Road scene from the Royal Liver Buildings is utterly transformed, bar the waters of Princes Dock. Gone are the B&I Line ferry, Liverpool Overhead Railway, Clarence Dock Power Station and countless warehouses

Above FISHY SITE: An unofficial fish market operated by Fleetwood traders sprang up by Clarence Dock in February, 1968, alongside Clarence Dock wall, part of engineer Jesse Hartley's scheme aided by John Foster and built by redundant soldiers after Wellington's Peninsula War

Top   NOT RUSHIN' – JUST MOORIN': Russian liner Viacheslav Molotov arrives in Liverpool with 791 seamen to take over 30 ex-German ships in British ports ceded to Russia as wartime reparations in January, 1946

Above EIGHT IN THE SHADE: Winter sunlight creates sharp shadows at Princes Dock one January morning in 1972, when Stephen Shakeshaft ventured out in a temperature of minus eight

ICONIC VIEW: Ocean yacht the Falmouth Packet passes along the city waterfront

Top   WAGON TRAIN: Railway fans pack out open mineral wagons as two saddle tank engines power this Wirral Railway Circle tour around
Birkenhead's dockland system, caught by Bob Bird approaching Canning Street in July, 1972

Above HATCHING PLANS: A white-shirted ship's dock boss instructs his hatchmen about unloading Blue Star Line's Iberia Star
(ex-Thysville, of Belgium), in Liverpool docks, June 1969

Top THIRSTY WORK: Canadian Pacific's postwar favourite, Empress of France, tops up her tanks from a bunker barge in Gladstone Dock, during March 1958, after her spring overhaul when she received cowl-topped funnels

Above BERTH PLAN: At Birkenhead on July 28, 1953, Anglo-Saxon Petroleum Co's newly launched tanker Hemidonax – the first of six sisters – is purposefully towed by Storm Cock into Cammell Laird's fitting out basin, aided by a ubiquitous gig boat

LOST WORLD: An eye-watering maritime scene at Princes landing stage with L&NWSSCo's St Tudno, left, loading passengers for Llandudno and Menai Bridge, while Cunard Line's Carinthia, right, is between Quebec-Montreal voyages in August, 1962. Passengers were probably more comfortable on Carinthia's transatlantic voyages with her stabiliser fins, whereas St Tudno was a notorious roller in the North Wales coast's westerlies. Time's water-winged chariot, though, was calling on such seemingly ageless sights. This was St Tudno's and the L&NWSSCo's last season and only five years later Carinthia closed Cunard's Liverpool to Canada service

GOING GREEN: The gorgeous Cammell Laird-built second Mauretania lies alongside in Gladstone Graving Dock, awaiting refit in December 1963, prior to a West Indies cruise. Airlines had stolen her traditional transatlantic business and Cunard painted her in Caronia-style green to aid her cruising appeal, but again she was outpaced by newer, flashier, purpose-built ships

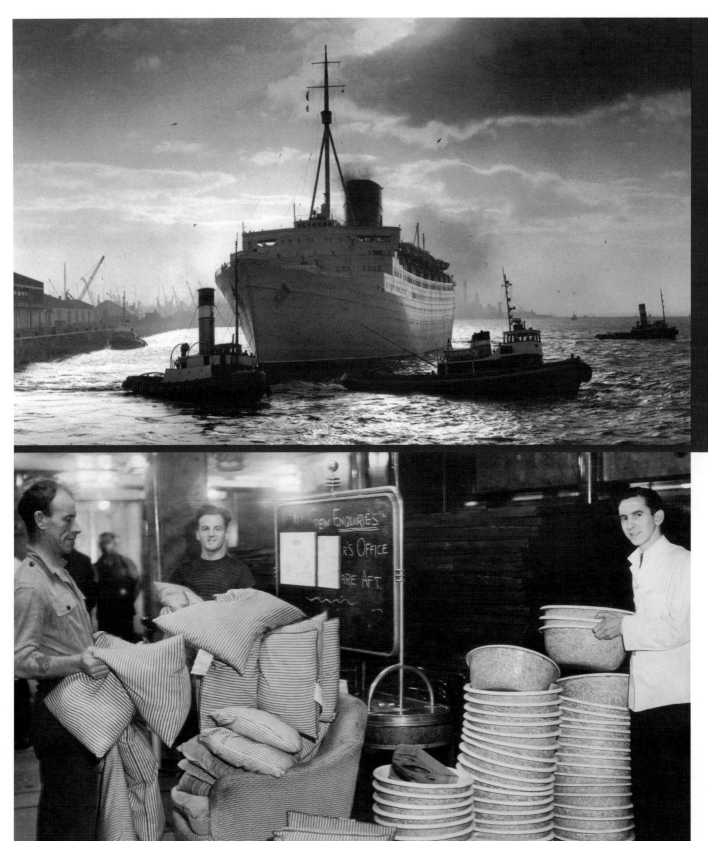

Top GREEN GODDESS: Cunard Line's great postwar dollar earner, "the millionaires' ship" Caronia leaves Gladstone Lock on a silvery Mersey and turns for Southampton and the West Indies, aided by Alexandra tugs old and new, in early January 1961, after an annual overhaul

Above DOCK BASIN: During an earlier refit at Cammell Laird, in September 1946, Mauretania undergoes the massive transformation from WWII troopship back to luxury liner, including the removal of baby baths after carrying hundreds of brides who had married Canadian soldiers

BATHING BELLES: Canadian Pacific pulls out the stops in April, 1957, with these models showing how to act naturally in the new Empress of England's swimming pool. The men, though, look as if they've been drafted in from accounts

Top HOME LEAVE: Soldiers move luggage from Britain's last troopship, Bibby Line's Oxfordshire, in March 1957, after docking at Princes landing stage, after carrying regiments home from the Suez crisis, in which the pram was probably very useful

Above SILVER SERVICE: Stewards prepare Empress of England's first class restaurant for her maiden voyage in April, 1957. The plain modern interior shows why there was such nostalgia for the older prewar liners – it was country house versus airport lounge style

HEAVE-HO: Officers high on the prow of the brand new Mauretania anxiously watch Thistle Cock and Holm Cock haul her bow around into Gladstone Dock to have her rudder fitted in May, 1939

TOWERING STEEL: Big and beautiful, the curvaceous "sharp end" of Empress of Canada rises like a cliff above inspecting officers in Canada Graving Dock, in Neville Willasey's record of her November, 1967 refit. The Canadian Pacific flagship once impaled a whale on this bulbous bow

GOLDEN GIRL: Was there ever a lovelier name for ship than Aquitania? Created to compete with White Star Line's Olympic and Titanic, Cunard's 1914 superliner brazenly reveals her derriere and four giant propellers in Gladstone Graving Dock, apparently built to accommodate her great bulk. Cunard responded by relocating the liner to Southampton

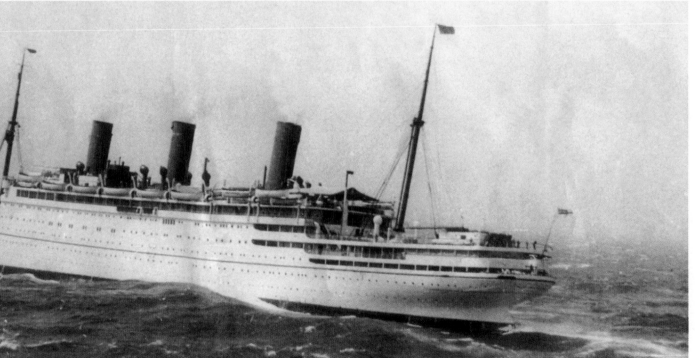

Top GOLDEN GIRL No 2: Cunard's mighty first Mauretania, Blue Riband of the Atlantic holder for 22 years until snatched by Germany's Bremen. Turning in the Mersey on May 24, 1924, after conversion to oil-firing and refitting in Gladstone Graving Dock, she proved to be faster than ever

Above GOLDEN GIRL NO 3: Canadian Pacific's Empress of Australia pitches and rolls in the Atlantic, while carrying King George VI and Queen Elizabeth on a state visit to North America, in May 1939. The photo was taken from the white empress's escort, the battle-cruiser HMS Repulse, which also picked up Royal pictures taken aboard and dropped overboard in a barrel for collection. Such was pre-internet life

EAGLE'S EYRIE: The sign aboard this Wallasey steam ferry warns that "Passengers are forbidden to speak to the officers of this vessel underway".
Well, would you risk it?

Top SAFETY FIRST: Capt Dobson contemplates his new charge Empress of Canada, in April, 1961. The latest electronics apparently
made her the safest ship afloat, so why so many life-jackets piled along the bridge front?

Above MARINE MINIATURES: Liverpool Museum's superlative ship model collection awaits transfer to public display from the Bootle warehouse,
after the war. They're now back there, in spite of having a Merseyside Maritime Museum

Top COAL HOLE: A suspiciously unsweated stoker, sporting a clean vest, demonstrates some spade work in a cold-looking furnace down in the engine room in May, 1955, aboard one of the Mersey's numerous steam tugs

Above BOMBED OUT: Liverpool Museum craftsmen Albert Hale, left, and John Shannon, rebuild a model of Royal Mail Line's Arlanza, in February, 1959, some 18 years after being Blitz damaged

HOMEWARD BOUND: Manx ex-pats from the US and Canada return to the island via Cunard's Ascania, far left, which called especially at Douglas for the party, who are seen being tendered ashore via IoMSPCo's Snaefell, in June, 1952. Clearly, they've prospered while in North America

OLD FAITHFULS: IoMSPCo contactors (season ticket-holders) Robert Thomson and H S Ross can't hide their disappointment aboard the magnificent 1930 Lady of Mann that their favourite ship faces imminent withdrawal

Top WOGGLE SQUAD: US Scouts arrive at Liverpool aboard Canadian Pacific's Duchess of York in July, 1929 for the International Jamboree, and chat with Lord Hampton of the Scouts HQ staff, fourth from right

Above SPECIAL CARGO: Liverpool's celebrated boxer Dom Volante strides down Cunard White Star M/V Britannic's crew gangway in December, 1954, where he was a fixture in the liner's gym after retiring from the ring

Top GONE FISHING: Liverpool's last fisherman John Neary sits on the quayside of Cockle Hole, less than a mile from the Pier Head, with his nobby boat, Comrade, moored behind, in January 1961

Above NEW DAWN: Mr and Mrs William Ordish, from Leigh, Lancashire, and their family, Brian, 11; Joan, 18; Doreen, 14; and Jean, 6, with a doll big enough to need its own berth, were six of the 2,010 emigrants who boarded Cunard White Star's M/V Georgic at Princes Landing Stage, departing for Australia on January 11, 1949

MASTER COMMANDER: Capt Thomas Corteen, on Lady of Mann's bridge, prior to her withdrawal in August 1971. Capt Corteen was her regular master in latter years, regarded as the best at handling a reputedly sensitive ship

DOWN BELOW: Chief engineer John Paynter of Wallasey waits for orders from the bridge on L&NWSS Co's St Seiriol en route to Llandudno
and Menai Bridge in May, 1959. He could tell the ship's position from commands on the engine room telegraph behind him

Top   COMEDY SERVICE: Returning home form Canada, Liverpool comedian Tommy Handley, star of the wartime hit radio show ITMA, demonstrates a tea tray routine to Liverpool's Lord Mayor and entourage aboard a Canadian Pacific liner at Princes landing stage in August, 1949

Above TIME'S UP: As the evening draws on, two Pier Head regulars trade some wry recollections during demolition of the original Mersey Ferries' George's landing stage, in April, 1973

FOR THOSE IN PERIL ON THE SEA

Top   FLY PAST: Supermarine Attacker jets – the Royal Navy's first jet type – of the Northern Air Division, RNVR, stage a mock attack on the
seaward defence vessel HMS Dee, during the Combined Naval Regatta at Otterspool Promenade, in July, 1955

Above MARCH PAST: Flag-waving crowds welcome back members of the King's Regiment (Liverpool) as they disembark from a troopship at
Princes landing stage and march, with bayonets fixed, out of Princes Parade in March, 1955, after three years' service in Hong Kong and Korea

Top   FLAG DAY: Plenty of activity at the Royal Naval Volunteer Reserve's Mersey Division Navy Day on June 22, 1957, with HMS Mersey, left, the division's coastal minesweeper, and club boat, HMS Eaglet, right, with Albert Dock warehouses behind

Above   FLOATING FORTRESS: Pushed by the tug Prairie Cock, the battleship HMS King George V, with funnels covered, leaves Gladstone Dock after overhaul in August, 1955, to join the reserve fleet. She was the penultimate battleship to visit Liverpool (HMS Vanguard was the last)

KILLER WHALE: HMS Courageous, one of the Royal Navy's hunter-killer submarines, visits Royal Seaforth Dock in August, 1976. But even a £75m super-submarine needs a humble little gig boat to take her mooring lines in the method employed since ancient times

6 9

Top LANDING STRIP: A convoy of US planes delivered for the war effort pass along Liverpool Strand

Above TROOP SHIP: Six months after war ended, soldiers pack quay and ship Orient Line's Orion on a rare visit to Liverpool, in December, 1945

FOR THOSE IN PERIL ON THE SEA

Top   RUNAWAY: Capt Johnnie Walker's former command, the sloop HMS Stork, of the Liverpool-based U-boat hunter killer Second Escort Group, is moored at Princes landing stage in February, 1954, after breaking free while being towed across the Irish Sea for lay-up. It is hoped to preserve Stork's sister ship Whimbrel in Liverpool as the Battle of the Atlantic Memorial Ship

Above CHASE AFOOT: Capt Johnnie Walker shouts encouragement from HMS Starling to nearby crew aboard HMS Woodpecker, on his most successful U-boat patrol when he sank six submarines

Top JOB DONE: The First Lord of the Admiralty, A V Alexander, welcomes home the massed crews of Johnnie Walker's Second Escort Group after they had sunk 17 U-boats

Above HIDDEN MENACE: After surrendering, German submarine U-532 carrying 150 tons of cargo from Japan to Germany, is escorted through Gladstone Lock, Liverpool, by frigate HMS Grindall, in May, 1945

Top   GLORIOUS GLOSTERS: Men of the 1st Battalion Gloucester Regiment march along Princes Landing Stage to board on the troopship
Empire Halladale for Kenya, during the Mau-Mau uprising in March, 1955

Above COMMAND CREW: Battle of the Atlantic campaign staff from the Western Approaches HQ, "The Citadel" located beneath Derby House,
Liverpool, photographed outside Liverpool Cathedral, with their chief, Admiral Max Horton, seated left

DEDICATED SERVICE: The Merchant Navy Memorial is dedicated at Liverpool Pier Head in November, 1952, with Liverpool Corporation fire boat William Gregson behind

FIRE SHIP: Training ship HMS Conway, the venerable Nelsonian "wooden-walls", is hosed down after being wrecked and catching fire in the Menai Straits through incompetence, in October, 1956

Top ROCK BOTTOM: The freighter Gusel sits on the bottom after a collision in fog off Rock Ferry in January, 1957
Above ENGINE BUILDERS: Cammell Laird machine shop engineers pause, in December, 1938, while building the steam turbine engines and casings for Cunard's second Mauretania, which powered her faultlessly several times around the world in peace and war

FULL RIG: With the drop in ship building orders in the 1970s, Cammell Laird turned to oil and gas rig production. The giant Sovereign Explorer floats out of the Birkenhead yard in this Stephen Shakeshaft picture, attended by Alexandra tugs Salthouse and Wallasey. The launch was marred by the death of a shipyard worker when a steel hawswer snapped

BIG COG: Teeth on the huge auxiliary turning wheel of the Cunard transatlantic liner Mauretania's steam turbine engine gears gets a final rub in Cammell Laird's machine shop in December, 1938

Top HELPLESS: The tug Grebe Cock, a naval whaler and motor boat stand-by impotently at the protruding stern of the submarine HMS Thetis which sank on trials in Liverpool Bay on June 2, 1939

Above FALSE HOPE: Meanwhile anguished relatives at Cammell Laird shipyard gates receive the false news that the sub is safe, whereas only four survived out of 103 crew and visitors onboard after a hatch jammed

FISH-SHAPE: More Henry Moore abstract sculpture than submarine, the curvaceous HMS Porpoise gets at hose-down in Seaforth while being overhauled

Top CHIPPING AWAY: Some of the finest furniture joiners and craftsmen were once employed in British shipyards. Here's Cammell Laird's carpenters' shop in 1938 working on furniture and fittings for Cunard's Mauretania

Above QUESTION TIME: How many workers does it take to change a ship's propeller? Five men ponder at the business end of Mauretania's propulsion. We'll ignore the obvious health and safety issues apparent here

GREAT ARK: The vast bulk of the aircraft carrier HMS Ark Royal slips into her natural element at Cammell Laird shipyard, Birkenhead, in May, 1950, after launching by HM Queen Elizabeth (later Queen Mother), in this splendid Neville Willasey view

Top MISSING GRACE: Both the Royal Liver Building, left, and Port of Liverpool Building are complete, but Cunard Building is yet to fill the gap in this July 1913 picture of crowded ferries attending King George V's visit to Liverpool

Above WEIGHTY MATTER: Normally the preserve of liners and large ferries, the Liberian tanker Vermont makes an unusual sight at Princes landing stage, moored to lighten her load from the Dutch West Indies to enable transit of the Manchester Ship Canal, in August, 1970

Top   COME RAIN: Two equally familiar views of George's landing stage for the Mersey ferries, firstly as it lies near deserted, wind and rain swept in June 1946
Above COME SHINE: Scores of Wirral-bound cyclists board the steam ferries for Birkenhead, Wallasey and New Brighton (the white funnel is Royal Iris II) in April, 1954, with Cunard Line's Franconia further along Princes landing stage

IN A SPIN: Dock board big-wigs mull over the new Mersey Bar lightvessel Planet tied up at Princes landing stage after high winds thwarted attempts by Vigilant (seen here) and Salvor to anchor her 12 miles out from Trafalgar Dock, in September, 1960. IoMSPCo's King Orry lies ahead

BIG SHED: Like George Formby with attitude, this fashionable young man, standing centre, unflinchingly gazes at the camera as a well-dressed crowd of holidaymakers wait patiently for the Isle of Man boat in the 1928-built Princes Parade waiting room, sometime during the 1930s

Top RUNNING REPAIRS: Men aboard a gig boat and pontoon maintain the Liverpool landing stages in October, 1969

Above KINDLY LIGHT: Oil flares guide the Birkenhead ferry Claughton alongside during a pea-souper fog in December, 1960

END IS NIGH: With the Mersey's glory days over, passengers for the Wallasey Ferries pick their way through demolition of the original Liverpool landing stages, in May 1973. Just like in 2007

BUSY BOAT: Plenty of well-turned out holidaymakers queue for to board IoMSPCo's Lady of Mann
(by then 30 years old) in July, 1960

TOP JOB: Sailors line the yard-arms of the Spanish training square-rigger Arc Gloria, in Richard Williams' August 1992 picture during the Tall Ships Race. The tradition of such a display on entering port was to indicate that the crew were not manning the guns